PREPARING
FOR A
LONG RIDE
When Distance Is the Goal

LEN CROW

WESTBOW
PRESS
A DIVISION OF THOMAS NELSON
& ZONDERVAN

WestBow Press books may be ordered through
booksellers or by contacting:

WestBow Press
A Division of Thomas Nelson & Zondervan
1663 Liberty Drive
Bloomington, IN 47403
www.westbowpress.com
1 (866) 928-1240

ISBN: 978-1-9736-2251-2 (sc)
ISBN: 978-1-9736-2250-5 (e)

Print information available on the last page.

WestBow Press rev. date: 03/28/2018

INTRODUCTION

Len Crow is no stranger to long distance riding. Since 1996 he has ridden over 32,000 miles on long distance journeys, including training, conditioning and pleasure riding.

Using his love for horses and his desire to help others, Len founded Ride for Missions in 1996, which would lead to life changing journeys on horseback to help mission works around the world.

In that year, he rode from Fairbanks, Alaska to El Paso, Texas, a distance of 4,200 miles. Two years later Len road 151 miles in 24 hours, non-stop, in a Pony Express type ride in the Salt Lake Desert. In 2002 he returned to Utah. Using 15 horses he rode 308 miles in 46 hours.

Seven other riders joined with him in 2005 to ride relay style from Emerson, Manitoba to the Calgary Stampede, a distance of 1,000 miles. They were then privileged to ride in the Stampede parade. A 50 mile historical trail facilitated four teams in another relay race.

The longest ride, from Deadhorse, Alaska, on the Arctic Ocean, to south of Guadalajara, Mexico was made in 2014-2015 and covered 7,000 miles. Len was in the saddle one year and four days.

The seventh Ride for Missions took place in Israel where Len was able to ride through the Judean desert.

As of the writing of this book, another long distance ride is in the planning stages for the fall of 2018 to ride the Trail of Tears from Telqua, Oklahoma to Cherokee, North Carolina.

These rides have given Len the ability to see some of the most beautiful country from the back of his horse. It has pushed both him and his horses to their limits as athletes. Meeting strangers who have become friends over the years and seeing the kindness of people as they helped him along his way has been such a blessing. Len will still say the most rewarding part of these rides is that they have enabled him to help orphanages in Cambodia, Philippines, Mexico, and the widows and children of fallen IDF soldiers in Israel.

Len and his wife Nancy have been married since 1975 and have 3 sons and 3 grandchildren.

Len is the founder and Pastor of North Country Baptist Church, Orillia, Ontario and the North Country Baptist Children's Home in Siem Reap, Cambodia. The orphanage recently celebrated it's 10th anniversary. There are 22 children currently being cared for in the facility.

As well as his duties of pastoring his church and running the orphanage, Len travels frequently to his many speaking engagements. The love of his life, next to his wife, Nancy, is to be on horseback exploring some new country side.

1

Personal Preparations

There is a certain glamour or fantasy that comes alive when talking to folks about a long- distance horseback ride. It would be a dream of many to do such a ride across the country. The experience of the wilderness and wildlife, the interesting people you meet and the achievement of pushing yourself to the limit when it is just you and your horse is what motivates people to consider it.

Your level of riding and training is important, but not everything. Personal skill will improve as you work on preparing your horse, gathering your tack and talking to others. There is no replacement for spending time in the saddle.

The first thing to think about is your goal. It is the easiest part but be cautious to make it your goal and not someone else's. Setting the goal may include a destination, an end and a starting point to satisfy a desire and accomplish the experience with your horse. Nothing is wrong with that. However, it has been several decades since I simply rode for pleasure. I found for me to accomplish my goal is to ride for a purpose, not just pleasure. But with that in mind, there is no disputing that the two do overlap. Riding to help others in difficult places has kept me in the saddle when it would be easy to throw in the towel.

I ride to raise awareness and money for widows and orphans in other countries where they have so much less than we do here in North America. My wife and I have helped other charities start orphanages in the Philippines, Mexico, and Guatemala. Since 2007 we have been operating our own orphanage in Cambodia. I have visited all of these countries and worked on their buildings, in most cases during the construction process. Having the pictures in my mind of these children as I ride keeps me focused on completing my goal.

Setting your route is as easy as setting the two locations of a start and finish point on your map and then drawing a straight line between the two. After drawing the line from point A to B customize the course by avoiding things like lakes, mountain ranges, cities etc. River crossings will also play a part in mapping your route. I have generally adjusted my route as I go using local information.

Today's smart phones and G.P.Ss help immensely in your travels. My first ride in 1996 from Fairbanks, Alaska, to El Paso, Texas, was 6,700 km or 4,200 miles. I went to the Canada map office and bought $300.00 worth of topographical maps. Good planning, you would think. Well- turned out not so good. Most of the maps were outdated and could never account for forest fires that had completely obliterated the trail. Crisscrossing those areas of fallen, charred trees turned my grey gelding into a black horse. New logging roads and cut lines made these maps obsolete. My $300.00 investment only made good starter fuel for my campfire and coffee fires.

You may want to include specific points of interest as you plan your route. Setting your goal may be influenced by other people with good intentions but bear in mind you are the one riding so take the advice of others graciously but keep in mind your own objectives.

I never tell anyone that I am going to attempt to ride from point A to point B. I don't like the word attempt. It comes from the root word tempt or temptation. It sounds like something that could change if the going got tough. I like to say "I intend" to ride from point A to point B. No use setting yourself up for failure before you begin.

Character traits like determination, stubbornness and grit will help you finish your course. It is important to spend some time in self-evaluation. You need to also evaluate your physical condition. Heart problems, diabetes or other medical issues should be considered if you go it alone. With that being said, proper consideration for your horse is also important. A strong, healthy, happy horse will carry you to the finish line. One of my greatest joys is seeing new country on the back of a good horse. Consider a couple of things. Do you intend to make this ride alone, with someone else, or in a group setting? For me, most of my riding has been solo. At times I have had others join me and I was grateful to have the company. However, the more I rode the more I learned about myself and whether genetically or as an acquired trait, I found myself enjoying the solitude. The company is great but I am most content as a lone rider.

Consider the wildlife in the area you plan to travel. Although you can never fully prepare for every issue try to think through every possible obstacle in advance.

Let me share one of my experiences on my 6th Ride for Missions from Deadhorse, Alaska, to Mismaloya, Mexico.

As we were crossing the Brooks Range in Alaska I told my wife I wished to get away from civilization and would camp out for that night. She laughed because civilization was our two friends who were the support crew and herself. They were the only people within 200 miles in any direction.

I found a good place to camp about 300 feet from a medium sized stream that I could use for water. There was some grazing for my horse and a level spot for camping. I tethered my Arabian horse, Music, to a tree and started my campfire. I cooked a quick meal while my coffee boiled. I grained Music. My bedroll was unfurled and I used my saddle as a pillow. After checking my firearms I promptly fell asleep. One hour later Music woke me by blowing and stomping. In grizzly and black bear country you better come alive quickly. Music had seen a bear coming into camp 100 yards away and wanted me to wake. I always sleep with a firearm and knife under my bedroll. When I got up, my 12 gauge, sawed off 3" mag was in my hands. My shotgun was already loaded with slugs. I generally carry a 45-70 Marlin or my 44 magnum Winchester.

The bear was cautiously moving toward camp. This bear's ears were up and he was sniffing the air as he came closer. Weaving back and forth I believe the bear was curious about his new neighbour. I spoke to him, picked up my coffee pot, and added some pebbles to make lots of noise. It caught the bear's attention but he showed no sign of aggression so I set my coffee pot down and chucked a couple of rocks at him and the bear went looking for a friendlier camp. I laid back down and was soon asleep when an hour later Music again began to stomp. As the first time, I was instantly awake and up. This was a different bear. Slightly smaller with a white blaze on his chest, whether genetic or an old battle scar, I do not know. He was as curious as the first bear, testing the wind, weaving side to side, ears erect as he drew closer. Using the same technique with my coffee pot I chucked some more rocks, keeping my 12 gauge at the ready. Like bear number one he also left for more amicable company.

Before making camp, I had checked the area for tracks and found many bear, wolf and caribou tracks but not enough to constitute a game trail, although the stream close by would be a natural draw. In any event, I walked over to Music and stroked her neck to assure her all was well. The fire was dying so I piled on more wood then returned to my saddle and blanket. I was soon sleeping once again when in another hour Music started stomping and blowing again. I was up fast and instantly alert. There was movement about 60 yards away moving fast. A bear topped a rise and slowed. This bear was different than the first two, much larger and not curious. His ears were flat back and he was popping his teeth, making bluff charges and tearing the ground with his front paws. He slowed to a trot but not weaving or misdirected, he was coming straight towards me. I somehow felt myself wishing I was somewhere else, like Philadelphia right then. I tried the coffee pot routine but he was coming too quickly. I pumped a round into the chamber of my shotgun and tried shouting at him, then I tried talking calmly. He got in my comfort zone of about 12 feet when I fired a shot at his front paws hitting the gravel and dirt. He jumped back about 30 feet but then he came again, only slower but very deliberate. I couldn't believe he was coming back. He was a magnificent looking creature. It was mid-June but he was already fat and his coat was glistening under the midnight sun. I had already pumped a fresh round into the chamber but I didn't remember doing it. I replaced the spent shell with another into the magazine.

After carrying the shotgun for nearly 20 years loading was a reflex action. Again, I spoke gently to him explaining he needed to go back to his family or I would surely kill him or pepper spray him. Giving him one last chance, I hurled a rock with my left hand and gripped my 12 gauge in my right hand. At 20 feet the rock bounced off his shoulder and he veered away past Music and out of sight.

After 30 minutes curled up in my bedroll, sleep would not come so I broke camp and at 3 a.m. headed down the trail and back to civilization, or our little camp of 3 people.

It should be noted all three of these bears were black bears although the last one would have been 600 pounds and all three potentially dangerous. If any of these bears had of been a grizzly I would have left camp on the first encounter.

2

The horse

I have owned a variety of horse breeds and I believe every breed has its' super stars. The breed that I have chosen and almost exclusively use is the Arabian. They are tough and hearty. Having rode 32,000 miles on horseback the horses I have used are my heroes.

On average the Arabian has extremely hard feet, is gentle and intelligent, and has one less rib leading to a larger heart and lung capacity.

I am 5"8" tall, and for me a horse that is 14.3 to 15.2 hands is the range I prefer. I have been astride horses 17 hands tall but the smaller horse covers just as much ground. Since I do a lot of solo riding, if I have an accident, it is much easier to mount a shorter horse.

In 2014 on my ride from Alaska to Mexico my favorite horse, General, and I took a fall. I broke General as a 5 year old during my first ride in 1996. General is a 15.2 Arab gelding and I have had 2 major wrecks with him, neither of them was his fault. The first was an error of judgement while the second was a deal that just happened.

General and I were out early and making good time in the flat country. I finished an early coffee over an open fire and felt mighty good in the cool morning air with the scent of pine in every breath. General was trotting at a fast pace and I could tell he too was feeling good, when he stepped into a hole on the side of the road no more than 6" deep with his lead foot. He tried to regain his balance by swinging his front leg forward. I have never seen blacktop like that on this road. It was very coarse with rocks sticking up 1/4 to 3/8 above the asphalt. General's effort to catch his balance failed when his shoe caught that rough surface and he did a somersault. I was caught completely off guard and went over his head. In an effort to avoid crushing me he tried to throw himself sideways which likely spared me from very grave injuries. In the process he hit his head hard on the asphalt, tore his knee and hurt his right shoulder. I hit the asphalt sliding forward breaking my shoulder and tearing my rotator cuff as well as lacerating my elbow and chipping the bone. A shorter horse was much easier to mount after such a fall. General has fully recovered and is still used today for light riding at the age of 27.

As you embark on your ride you will learn more about your horse than you ever thought possible. The horse is a truly amazing creature. Monitor your horse and keep him or her in the best condition possible.

Learn the signs of dehydration or soring up from strains and twists. I have never in 42 years had an Arabian colic on me but it could happen, so ask your vet what to do and what to look for.

Have your vet evaluate your horse before your ride to be sure he is in top condition. Crossing state or provincial lines and certainly country borders will require a proof of ownership and a veterinarian certificate of good health including up to date vaccinations. If your horse is over 10 years old I recommend having your horse's teeth checked to see if floating is necessary. If you are purchasing a horse for your trip it is a good idea to have it vet checked if you are unfamiliar as to what to look for. A horse with a longer back will generally give you a smoother ride. Look for a straight line from withers to tail along his back. Having higher withers is not always a bad thing, it certainly does help to keep your tack in place. A horse that is overweight and too round will cause you to be constantly adjusting your saddle. After several hundred miles this should no longer be a problem!

Check the feet for cracks from the coronet band down or the toe up. Lift up the foot to check the frog and sole. Take a hoof pick along and look for signs of founder and laminitis, where the hoof wall separates from the sole. There is no point in starting your ride handicapped with a lame horse as you head down the trail.

I generally look for smaller head. A horse built for distance will have bright eyes that are alert and kind.

The horse's coat should be shiny. A waxy feeling coat usually means a horse is low in minerals or vitamins.

If it is late spring and the horse has an uncommonly long coat that is lasting longer than others that have shed their coats already, it is again a sign of low minerals over the winter months.

Look for nice straight legs and run your hand down the leg for signs of swelling, wind puffs or deformities. If you are looking at a thoroughbred, check the ankles for multiple dark dots that usually mean the horse has been pin fired.

Watch the horse as he moves around the round pen or corral. Does the level of his back remain the same as he moves? This may determine a smooth ride as compared to a jack hammer ride.

You want to avoid a horse that is flighty and spooks at everything but at the same time you do not want a horse so desensitized they no longer react to danger.

Think like your horse. When riding from the back country into a small town or city you may have some challenges. Going through a drive through for coffee with a horse that has never seen his reflection in a plate glass window may cause him to jump sideways so stay alert. Make this a time of wonderful memories for you and your horse.

You will need to determine if a pack horse will be necessary for your trip. My rule of thumb: If I am going to be more than 3 days between supply posts a pack horse is a good idea. You will want some practice if you have never tagged a horse with you. Make sure your lead rope to the pack horse doesn't cross under the tail of your saddle horse. You will find yourself in an impromptu rodeo ending with most of your gear spread across the great divide.

I usually plan on 3 to 4 months of conditioning for both my horse and me. Below is a similar plan to what I use in my horse preparations. The speeds will be inverted as the days of conditioning progress. Training will be 5 or 6 days a week. We have 1 hour and 10-minute sessions.

Week 1: 45 minutes at a walk, 10 minutes at a trot, 5 minutes at a lope and finally 10 minutes at a walk again.

Week 2: 15 minutes at a walk, 35 minutes at a trot, loping for 10 minutes and finally slowing to a walk for the final 10 minutes.

Week 3: A warm up walk of 10 minutes followed by 35 minutes of trotting, 15 minutes of loping and back to a walk out of 10 minutes.

Week 4: The beginning 10 minute walk, 30 minutes trotting time and 20 minutes loping followed by a cool down walk for 10 minutes.

Week 5: The usual 10 minute warm up walk with a 30 minute trot, 15 minute lope, then a 5 minute full out gallop and a cool down walk for 10 minutes.

Week 6: A 10 minute start up walk, followed by 30 minutes at a trot, 10 minutes at a lope and 10 minutes at a gallop. Finally, 10 minutes to cool down at a walk.

By the 6th week you will see significant improvement in muscle tone in both your horse and yourself. For the next 6 to 10 weeks increase the exertion level as your horse is able. This is a generic equation as each horse will progress at different levels. I have one horse that would not have it another way but to lope for a full hour on the first week!

Stretching your horse's legs is helpful before you ride. Lift the foot gently and extend the leg by adding support with your free hand. Do not rush the process, but with soft, gentle pressure the horse will give you his leg. Extend as far as is comfortable for the horse but do not over extend as the horse will lose his balance. After your workout rub your horse down before turning him loose. I keep my horse from drinking for 10 minutes after exercising to keep him from cramping up.

Vary the ground your horse will cover in this training process. The first week or two train on level, firm, but not hard surfaces. Later use open farm fields that are soft or sandy areas. Do not, however, push a horse in soft soil when he is getting tired.

After the first week try some hill climbing, gentle slopes and inclines as your horse improves.

Try to expose your horse to everything you may experience on the trail.

Ride over and along railway tracks. Take him to a small creek or stream and ask him to cross it. It may take some time but be patient. If you are training with a buddy, that horse may have no problem with the water and your timid one will follow the example of another horse. Let your horse get used to livestock by riding back roads or concessions. This will help when you encounter wildlife along your trip. The limited traffic on these roads are a help since rural folks tend to slow down when passing you. In these country settings you may flush a bird or rabbit which will help your horse get used to the suddenness of something moving or flying up quickly in front of him. When you ride through brushy areas never completely relax as a deer, elk, or bear may appear causing your horse to jump sideways. You in turn, may end up on the ground or worse with a torn groin muscle. Your horse should get used to wooded areas where he must walk over fallen trees and logs and wind his way through the forest.

In a controlled setting you may want to try swimming with your horse or choose a steep, sandy incline to ride down. Make sure you lean back in the saddle and push forward in the stirrups. Keep the horse's head straight downhill. Coming down a hill sideways may cause the horse to lose his balance or footing and topple.

These are some suggestions meant to increase your horses' physical strength as well as introduce him to experiences he will face along your journey.

I do not recommend that you condition more than 3 horses at a time. I have had others help me condition horses which has reduced my work load. A buddy also gives you someone to ride with if you live close by each other.

Len Crow

Your horse's good conditioning will allow him to ride calmly in many different circumstances.

3

Your tack

Next to your horse, your tack will be the most significant part of your trip. You will need to determine how long you will be between supply posts, whether from a city, town, village or your own support crew. I use a support crew so my wife can be involved with my projects. I generally travel light but at times a pack horse has been helpful. The X frame pack saddle is the best, with double panniers, one on each side and a top pack in the middle. There is an alternative that is a 2 pannier design to fit over your extra riding saddle.

I do not recommend you buy a new saddle for your trip unless you do not have one yet. If you must buy a new one, you will want to get as many miles as you can astride the saddle to break it in.

The new leather makes a lot of creaking noise at first. It can be eliminated by using leather oils to soften the new, stiff leather.

Let's first take a look at your saddle then we will consider the other tack.

Personally, I use a western, Circle Y, endurance saddle with a horn. I also have a Ken McNabb all round roping saddle and a Billy Cook Pleasure saddle. The Circle Y saddle has 31,000 miles that I have put on it. I use it the most as it fits me like a glove. Next to the Circle Y my choice would be the Ken McNabb saddle. The first time I sat in it felt like I had used it for years. The Australian saddle and English saddles are good for certain applications or perhaps shorter rides. You want your saddle to fit your horse to avoid soring him up. I use a light blanket then a saddle pad under my saddle to ensure more comfort for my horse and to keep my saddle pad clean. It is easy to wash out a thin saddle blanket in a stream or lake and have it dry in a day. The saddle pad takes a much longer time to dry and the fibre tends to break down more quickly. There are some laundry mats that have industrial machines that will allow you to wash and dry your horse blankets, but check first. My choice of doubling up using a saddle blanket and pad has another application. I have had to sleep in a snow bank with nothing more than my slicker, saddle and saddle pad.

I use 6 saddle strings on my saddle about 3' in length to tie my gear in place. These stay supple and pliable for tying if you make a point of oiling them often. There are many prepared leather oils but these can get pricey so I often use peanut oil. I like my saddle relatively plain with not a lot of tooling. This makes it much easier for maintenance and cleaning. The tooling also tends to hold rain.

My saddle has deep swales to suck my knees up to in the case where I am challenged by a bucking horse. I like a solid horn if I need to rope and pull something. Common sense will help the saddles' longevity. If you are riding a 900 or 1,000 lb. Arabian don't tie hard to your saddle horn if you plan to rope a 2,000 lb. bull. When your lighter Arab decides to shut it down you may end up being dragged around by the bull who might be just as indignant about the whole matter.

On my first ride in 1996 from Fairbanks to El Paso my family travelled the route by faith trusting God to meet our needs. Our boys learned to fish along the way for our supper. In the back country I would come across berry patches. Of course there was sometimes competition for the sweet tasting berries. The local bears enjoyed them too. My horse and I would charge the bears in question and drive them temporarily away so I could quickly fill a couple of containers and store them in my saddle bags to bring home to my family. I always tied the reins of my horse loosely to my belt for a speedy departure when the bears figured out they had been tricked.

One day in northern British Columbia I was slightly bored, and with many miles behind me it came upon me to have some fun and try and rope one of these bears. I chose a young 3 year old about 250 pounds and made my play urging General forward. Since he was used to chasing these bears, General lunged into action while I shaped my loop with my lariat. Moments later the bear dove into the thick, dense brush about 15 feet high. The bear simply put his nose to the ground and plowed through it. I relaxed in the saddle thinking the game was over but General dropped his head and plowed through after the bear. Now this game was getting trickier all that time. I clung to the saddle horn and pulled my knees up under the swales of my saddle and hung on. First my hat was dragged off my head. It was held only by the hat string which was pulling hard at my throat. I was glad I had on leather chaps and gloves. My face and neck were scratched and bleeding and I was grateful I had a bandana on to help protect my neck. My lariat was dragging behind me when General broke through the brush just in time see the little bear climb straight up a tree. To our dismay there was a big boar bear watching the circus from the base of the tree. He was not amused and he woofed and lunged forward stopping General in his tracks. It didn't take General long to make up his mind to retreat in reverse through the brush patch. My hat, still tied, was now hanging off my face and the back of my neck was getting scratched. I was glad for my leather vest. We broke free from the brush and feeling this game was getting a little western for him, General spun around and galloped the other direction with my lariat and the bear trailing behind. My concern was that the bear might step into the loop of the lariat or the loop get caught on a tree. Thankfully neither happened and I came away with an empty loop and a head that looked like I had fought a mountain lion.

The moral of the story is choose a saddle with deep swales, a strong horn and leave the bears alone!

I like a deep seat and high cantle when riding in the mountains. It helps keep you in the saddle when climbing. I also have a Mexican saddle that has a horn the size of a small steering wheel. I have thought of carving out a 3"x5" rectangle and dropping in a flush mounted G.P.S like the Garmin I use in my pickup truck. Unless your horse came with an accessory electrical plug in (which would only happen if you purchased the horse outside Wal-Mart that requires 25¢ to ride) then you would need to purchase a solar blanket to put over your rear saddle bags. You could also install running lights back there if you wanted to get really high tech. Since I am old school I still carry my compass and cell phone.

I have a hoof pick sheath on my outside rear latigo for easy access. If your saddle is older, check the fleece underside. It is relatively inexpensive to replace it if it is getting worn. Mine has been replaced twice by our local Mennonites with great results. Check your stirrups and fenders for thinning and wear and replace if they are questionable. Examine the tree on your saddle to make sure there is no give. Stirrups for endurance riding are very comfortable with a 1" of compressible foam. I recall the first time using them was like riding on air. I have regular leather stirrups and twisted stirrups that reposition the angle of your knees, making for a more comfortable ride. The cushioned endurance stirrups come in metal and plastic. The plastic ones are approximately a half pound lighter which may not seem like much but you will see that every pound matters to your horse. If you choose to try the twisted stirrups, bear in mind they will cost you nearly double compared to conventional stirrups but they are well worth the cost if you are having knee trouble.

Tapadaros are helpful for cold weather riding and riding in heavy brush. They protect your feet and prevent twigs from poking into the stirrups and jabbing your horse in the ribs. They also help block the wind. Leather, vinyl or heavy plastic are the usual materials they are fabricated from. Some are very ornate and decorated with silver conchos.

Consider the weight of your saddle. My Circle Y saddle is 23 pounds before my extra gear. The Ken McNabb saddle is nearly 40 pounds and is much more substantial. Every pound will count if you are planning to travel far. The Circle Y, for example, is 23 pounds. I weigh 175 pounds. My extra gear includes my boots, spurs, saddle bags, 2 firearms and cartridge belt with 3 knives, food for me and the horse, spare shoe, easy boot, water canteen (1 in the north 2 for in the desert) camera, field glasses, coffee pot with 2 cups (one for a guest), slicker, bedroll, hat, leather chaps, vest, phone and lariat. I reckon you get my point that weight starts to add up quickly. Every pound matters. I tried to trim my personal weight down to 165 or 170 before I ride but putting it all together your horse will be carrying 260-280 pounds. That is about 25% of his body weight.

There are lighter saddles that weigh as little as 15-25 pounds but my observation with these new finer saddles is that they do not stand up to the rigors of travel as do the leather ones.

When it comes to extra gear, I like to use what is familiar to me as it is tried and tested. There will be enough obstacles without trying new gear to see if it works. My Circle Y saddle has zero padding on the seat so on my second last ride in 2014-2015, I broke down and bought a gel seat cover. Laugh if you will, but if I am going to be doing 50 or 60 miles in a day I like it. As to the other gear, much will come down to personal comfort and preference.

My saddle is my work bench. I carry one canteen with 1.5 litres of water in areas with easy access to water and in the desert I carry a 2 litre canteen. Make note as you load your gear onto your saddle of the weight distribution or your saddle will tend to turn on you. I use a fleece front cinch and a leather back cinch. If your saddle does not have a back cinch you should have one installed. Coming down a steep bank or riding along the side of a mountain you don't want the saddle tipping forward onto your horse's neck and putting your horse dangerously off balance. Also, you will likely lose the saddle pad and blanket out the back door and not even notice it immediately. The same applies to the breast collar. If you don't have one you will want to purchase one. Some saddles are equipped with a D ring screwed into the tree for you to fasten the breast collar to. While this might look good for parades and such it is not a good idea when it comes to extreme riding. You can purchase a leather strap that goes under the saddle horn and up and over the swales in front of the seat. I cross mine and fasten to the breast collar. This will give you maximum strength for climbing steep inclines and cause you less embarrassment by having your saddle slide back and again throwing your horse off balance.

Back to my canteen. In the desert I carry 2 canteens which give me 3 liters of water. On my 1996 ride I had traded a saddle for a spare horse. The mare was just taken from a foal when I got her and she was still producing milk. I continued to milk her for the next two months so I would carry my Tim Horton's coffee mug and drink horse milk and give the water to my horse.

Always keep the canteen full. It may save your life in the desert. I carry my canteen fastened on the saddle horn for easy access.

A slicker is another thing I carry rolled up behind my saddle with my bedroll inside tied with a leather strap. I don't always have the bedroll on board, sometimes just the slicker. My slicker is not water resistant, it is water proof with a high fleece collar for cold weather riding. I carry leather saddle bags at the back under my slicker and leather pommel bags at the front of my saddle that fit over the horn. When using front pommel bags my canteen strap goes on first, then my pommel bags, then I tie one of my leather straps over and around the saddle horn. This ensures in an emergency, if you go into a gallop or get into a bog or quicksand you won't lose them. In my front pommel bags I keep my camera, binoculars, energy bars, rain cap for my cowboy hat, an extra hoof pic, lighter, sunglasses, maps and literature about my trip and anything else I need to access without getting out of the saddle. Rear saddle bags are larger and my metal coffee pot goes in there. I take the inner mechanism out of the pot and put in a bag of coffee, enough for one week, two cups then a wash cloth with the lid on top. The cloth keeps the jingling sound down and can be used as a towel for bathing in the rivers. The cloth is small, packs small and dries quick.

I pack enough grain for 2 days for my horse and enough food for me for the same amount of time. My camp hatchet is small, light, has a hollow handle and is as sharp as a razor. I also pack fire starter, a dinner plate and occasionally a small gold pan in place of the dinner plate to do double duty. I carry a 4 foot length of leather, and a spare horse shoe or easy boot. In my hatband I tuck 6 horseshoe nails in case I have to replace a thrown shoe. There is also a small medical bag as well as my lead rope and halter in the saddle bag.

My lariat is tied on the right side of my saddle, then I attach my two firearms, one on each side. A leather scabbard holds my guns. I wear a cartridge belt with 2 knives and a leatherman, my mini mag light and a zippo lighter in a leather sheath. I do not carry a wallet in my back pocket for obvious reasons plus I'd have a sore back in two days. My money is kept in my hatband inside my hat as well as my identification. Now you know why cowboys prefer to wear their hats everywhere rather than leave them lying around. I also carry bear spray and a snake bite kit in my saddle bags plus insect repellent during summer months and hand warmers in the cold months.

Your reins can be leather, nylon or rope. I choose leather. I like the solid rein but not so heavy as to put undue pressure on the mouth, so the medium weight leather is my choice. I prefer long reins. The leather reins give good grip when wearing gloves. The nylon type tends to slide. Braided works well for grip but the downside is that they hold water when riding in the rain. I like my reins long enough to have control when I dismount. By the way, I teach my horses to allow me to dismount from left, right, rear and over the head. When mountain riding on an eyebrow of a trail, you would understand why.

Consider a lighter bit and bridle if you chose to use them. Riding 100 miles in a day with a heavy bit and bridle on a horse could feel 10 times heavier to your horse's mouth by the end of the day. Remember a steel bit in -30 degree weather can freeze the corners of the horse's mouth. I use a curb or snaffle bit depending on the horse. In case of emergency I want maximum control. On one of my stallions, Jerbob, who is gone now, I used a hackamore. This can help if you want your horse to graze from time to time.

I have also used a bit less bridle given to me by Sherri Raguth who is a dealer for them. They are very gentle on the horse and again the horse has the freedom to graze. You will not have mouth problems with this system and they also come in leather or an incredibly strong vinyl. A bozel can also be used but my preference is the bit less bridle, again depending on the horse. My horse General is exclusively bit less while Dakota and Music are bit and bridle.

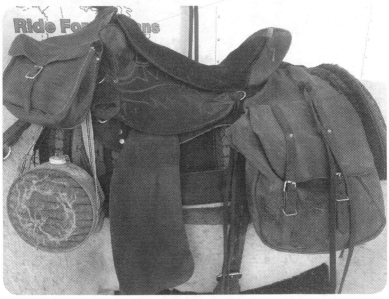

General with bit less bridle and my saddle with gear attached
ready to go.

4

Foot wear for you and your horse

I wear regular cowboy boots with a narrow toe for the ease of slipping into the stirrups. I like a high heel to keep my foot from going too far forward into the stirrup and an extended heel shelf to accommodate my spurs. My boots are leather and offer protection to the ankle in the saddle and on the ground. In rattlesnake country I like my high top, leather cowboy boots with leather chaps that go down over the top of the boot. I also wear my jeans over the top of the boots so nothing can fall down inside.

I seldom sleep in a tent or a sleeping bag when riding as I like to be up and ready at a moments notice. I usually do not remove my boots unless at the base camp where I sleep in the living quarter of our horse trailer. If you remove your footwear at night always, always, always shake them out before pushing your feet down into them. Your boots or footwear make a warm, safe haven for creatures looking for a safe place to spend the night. This is not as crucial during the winter but I still do so out of habit even in basecamp. I also wear moccasins to give my feet a rest.

This footwear works for me. The cowboy boots I use have a neoprene sole, not leather. This keeps my feet drier during wet weather. The leather soles will wick water right into your socks. In the winter I wear insulated riding boots. After riding through a blizzard in Montana with winds of 70 mph and - 50F, both my horses got frostbite and so did I in my feet and hands. The next day my wife was adamant that I spend the money on good winter riding boots that were rated for -40F. The boots I found were Kenetrek boots designed for cowboys. They still have the narrow toe, high heel and spur shelf. I insulated my tapaderos with sheepskin as well.

For my horse I use three systems as the terrain changes. I go bare foot in soft soil, steel plates in the rocky country and easy boots when road riding on asphalt or concrete, particularly in the cities or on the occasion I have gone into a building or gym to play basketball with some kids!

The easy boots are essential for me. I have lost a couple but if they are fitted properly then it is rare. They protect the frog and sole and hoof wall in gravel and slick or volcanic rock that can be very sharp. They cushion the horse's steps on hard surfaces to alleviate shin splints, wind puffs and sores. The care of your horse's feet will be the success of your ride. Happy feet, happy horse, happy, happy cowboy.

A barefoot horse in the Rocky Mountains will not last two days but with easy boots they protect during the day and can come off at night allowing the foot to relax, breathe and be refreshed. Use your hoof pick often to check for stones and bruising. In sand and soft soil your horse can travel hundreds of miles barefoot. Steel shoes last me 250 miles and if you are travelling at times 300 miles a week that means you have to shoe weekly. You will not have much of a hoof wall left. Easy boots last 450 miles and puts no strain or damage on the hoof wall.

As a side line; my average distance as I calculated it at the end of my rides was 23-24 miles per day. In the Rockies where there is a lot of climbing, river crossings and canyons you may only get 15 miles a day. In the desert or foot hills you can often go 60-70 miles. My average distance in Mexico was 36 miles per day.

I do not recommend borium weld for this type of ride. The borium is much harder than the steel shoe. While the steel plates quickly wear down the borium doesn't and tends to tip the shoe out of balance. I sored up two of my horses to learn this and I've never used it again. Regular steel toes and heels are a better choice in my way of thinking.

In rocky or gravelly areas plastic soles work well nailed in place under your shoe. The drawback, unlike easy boots; the sole and frog don't dry out. You can fill the void as I did with caulking to prevent mud or water from getting in there. This system does not allow the frog to be flexed as much in riding which pumps blood into the foot and is essential for hoof growth.

The good thing with the easy boots is that you can do a bi-weekly trimming to keep the foot at a constant length as opposed to regular farrier work every 6-8 weeks. If you are going to use steel plates keep some extra shoe nails with you and in a pinch you can use a rock or leatherman to correct a loose or thrown shoe. Keep in mind these supplies may be limited so I recommend you buy enough easy boots before you leave to keep with your support team or in the horse trailer. The equation I gave earlier- steel plates 250 miles and easy boots 450 miles will help you determine how many you will require.

If your horse develops a crack in his hoof I suggest you use steel shoes to hold it together. There is an epoxy compound you can use for horses to bind it together.

I need also mention I often use one size bigger in an easy boot and put it on top of a steel shoe when I go through a town or city.

Hoof flex painted on my horse's feet twice a week helps to keep them from drying out. A word of caution on this; put it on at night to give the hoof flex time to soak in or you may lose an easy boot to the greasy hoof surface.

5

Weather

After you have mapped out your trip, consider the terrain you will be crossing as well as the weather and seasons. It is interesting to me how many folks see a horse and rider going across country and in their mind it is always sunny with mild temperatures and the rain and snow only come at night. Your trip may only have pleasant weather about 30% of the time.

I have ridden through rain, sleet, hail, snow, blizzards, extreme heat, a tornado and a sand storm in the desert.

If you know you are going to be in winter weather adjust your route to minimize the time in the colder climate. Consider the starting and ending points and maybe instead of riding east to west ride west to east or instead of north to south ride south to north.

I have come very close to perishing in winter weather riding and although at times it can be pleasant it can turn real ugly on you.

I recall riding the high country in Idaho in 1996 and getting caught in a snow storm. In a matter of hours I lost the trail and had only a compass and map to navigate. That is a sure recipe for disaster as it is easy to ride off a cliff in the dark. I pushed on to lower elevation and managed by 2:00 am to get out of the mountains. In the dark I somehow missed my base camp and ended up sleeping in a snow bank with no more than my saddle pad, blanket and my slicker. In such cases if you can get out of the wind it will help. I dug out a section of a snowbank with my hands and made a hollow to crawl into. With the snow to insulate I was able to catch some sleep.

I wear long johns over briefs and a tee shirt, blue jeans and a regular shirt, leather chaps and vest and I keep my rain slicker on my saddle. I always wear a long sleeve shirt and long pants. That is my summer dress. For winter I add to that a sweater or down vest and a Carhart insulated coat. My cowboy hat is worn winter and summer but I keep a toque in my saddle bags for cold weather or sleeping at nights as 80% of body heat is lost through your head. I also carry a neck warmer. A bandana is also recommended. It will keep you cooler in summer and warmer in winter as well as protect from black flies, mosquitoes, and sunburn. It can also be used as a triangle sling, a filter for water, a bandage for wounds and I have used it as a mosquito netting by covering my whole head when I sleep to protect from insects. It has also been used as a flag to get someone's attention, a washcloth or towel when bathing in rivers or streams and a strainer for coffee grounds. Truly a versatile piece of clothing!

Two pairs of insulated gloves will be helpful as well. One pair to wear and one to keep should you lose a glove or gloves. Hand and toe warmers are a great idea if you have access to them. I wear my neck warmer up over my nose, mouth and ears in the biting cold and clip it under my hat at the back. My hat always has a hat string to ensure I don't lose it in the wind. I wear special winter boots which I mentioned in the previous chapter.

My canteens are filled at every opportunity. I have had them freeze solid in the north and in Mexico and Arizona the water got too hot to drink.

Winter blankets for my horse are kept at my base camp. My portable corral is set up to block wind using my horse trailer and truck. Also during cold weather I increase the horse's feed to keep them warm and energized.

Your horses feet will be a concern when you get into -30F weather. If you have shoes that are steel plates the ice will build up in the centre to a baseball size, solid ice ball so that your horse cannot stand. The ice will also build up inside your easy boots and cause them to gape at the top and pop off. The steel plates with plastic help a little but barefoot is the best. To remove the giant ice ball, I used a small saw and cut it off flat then dug out the balance, only to have to do it all again in an hour. Cutting the first ball is tricky because the horse will be teetering on high heels. At -50F and 70 mph winds on the flat lands in Montana there is bound to be trouble. The best you can do is find shelter for you and your horse. I was not able to get to shelter and both my horse and I got frost bite. The horse's skin froze where the wet edges of the saddle blanket touched but the worst was the front cinch area. Both sides froze and all the hair fell out in a 3"x8" patch on both sides. We stopped for a day till the winds stopped. My wife went to the nearest town and bought my winter riding boots and we put hoof flex on the bare skin of the horse to keep the skin soft without cracking. One week later the hair was growing in on the frozen areas. My gelding had frozen a spot on his nose but it also healed over nicely. The horses enjoyed their winter blankets that week.

Our team had a travel trailer and a horse trailer with living quarters. They had to be drained of water and winterized in the cold weather. All the horses water had to be kept in buckets in the trailers except the Lakota horse trailer as it had the water tank above the floor. The propane furnace plus a generator to run the electric heater kept the inside between 40-50F. Our water bottles froze beside our heads at night if sitting too close to the outside wall.

Black ice caused my mare to slip and I fell three times in one day until I could find a place to ride in snow for traction.

One small river crossing became more than a concern. I saw no alternative. It was running east to west and I was travelling north to south. This was in northern Wyoming and I decide to try crossing on the ice. I tied up my horse and first walked across myself. Jumping up and down on the ice it appeared to be solid. The river was no more than fifty feet across. I went back, untied Buddy, my gelding, and led him cautiously across. As we neared the bank there was a huge cracking sound and a piece of ice we were standing on tipped up in the air leaning toward shore. I jumped first and Buddy lunged right behind me. With his thrust the piece of ice cracked but he was still able to land six inches away from crushing me. He scampered up the bank dragging me with him as I held on to the reins.

A few months later, riding in Mexico, my water canteen was too hot to drink at 110F. My gear changed drastically. Riding in hot countries requires some sober thought. It can be as deadly as the harshest winter. Be certain to carry ample water. I generally carry 2, 1 1/2 litre canteens. There are areas you can find water for your horse but there are times you may have to be prepared to share your canteen. Most horses don't mind sharing as long as you let them drink first!

My hat turned upside down became a water bucket on occasion. I was able to find a tania in the desert rocks that would hold water for 3 or 4 days after a rain but they are not always accessible to your horse. You can sometimes find small streams or seeps that have been dug to form a pool. Be cautious if you come to a pool in the desert. A little oasis could be deadly if it is a saline pool. If your horse doesn't seem to want to drink, stay away. Look for obvious signs of other animal tracks. You will see these signs if the water is good. Approach with caution as there is the probability of quick sand near pools. You can look for bees flying in the air. They can lead you to water especially if you see several flying in the same direction. Toads or frogs don't wander far from water either.

There may be competition at the water holes or streams so stay alert. I recall riding up to a clean looking pool surrounded by tall grass and pond vegetation only to find myself in a snake pit.

In extreme heat, 100-120F you are better to ride in the early morning and evening or at night. Monitor your horse. Pinch his skin about 1". The skin will not bounce quickly back if the horse is becoming dehydrated.

If your pulse begins to race and you feel light headed, dizzy or nauseated and are not sweating you are in the beginning stages of heat stroke or exhaustion. It can kill you or your horse so take shelter. Stay in the shade to lower your temperature. Soak your bandana and drape it over the back of your neck. Keep a mental note as you ride of the water you may have passed. Scan the horizon for buildings or windmills, which in the desert, are usually standing above a stock tank filled with water. Both you and your horse need to keep your electrolytes up as you ride. Have drinks like Gator aid at your base camp. I always have a bottle of pills for leg cramps as this is an ailment that sometimes bothers me while working hard in the heat.

I used a product called Willard's water for my horse. It can be used for humans as well. This chemically processed water saturates and hydrates the vital organs very quickly.

A method I seen for the first time while riding in Mexico was a 2 litre bottle of electrolytes run interveinously into the horse. This is good for 2-3 weeks in hot weather.

While desert riding cross country stay focused on a landmark for your destination. The distance across the open desert is very deceiving. What looks like 5 miles could be 70.

A wide brimmed cowboy hat keeps the sun off your face and neck and gives shade to your eyes. Keep a whistle in your pommel bag if you need to get attention. It may bring help to you.

If you plan to camp overnight in the desert remember there is not much wood to burn. I make my fires with sagebrush or piñon. There is a certain brush like plant that is very poisonous. Using a branch to roast your hotdog could cause your death. Get to know poisonous plants growing in the area you plan to ride so you can avoid them.

When riding in Arizona and Mexico in particular watch for quick sand and slime pits. Riding in Arizona I stopped to evaluate the direction I was heading as I was off road. I noticed with my field glasses some crevices ahead about 200 feet away. These crevices can be 30 or more feet deep. When I lowered my glasses and looked down, my horse and I were standing on a 1" thick crust covering part of one of these crevices. I found myself wishing I was in Philadelphia or somewhere else! I wasn't sure what to do so I slowly backed my horse up the way I came until I was off the crust and made a very wide detour around the area.

Try to remain calm if you find yourself in quicksand. It helps if you do not struggle. Get clear of your horse as your horse will panic and be threshing with his front feet and you do not want to be hit by those flailing feet which could push you deeper in the quick sand.

I have twice been in quicksand and both my horses survived because I remained calm.

The first encounter with quicksand was a July 1st long weekend in Ontario. I set out early for a ride and after 4 hours I came to a flat bottom creek about 50 feet across. There was a 5 foot bank from where I was sitting and I figured my horse and I would drop over the edge of the bank and slide down into the water and walk easily across what seemed to be 6-8" deep water. My horse refused to budge. I used my spurs to edge him over the bank but he backed up. This was one of my biggest mistakes. I have since learned to listen to my horse. I tried to inch Patty, my horse, over the edge but instead of sliding down he bunched up and jumped off the 5' bank as if trying to jump to the other side of the 50' river. He jumped 15' feet from the bank and was immediately swallowed up to the girth in quick sand below the 6" of water. I rolled off to one side to lighten the weight on his back. Patty was panicking and thrashing his front feet forward. I was concerned he would hit me with one of his feet so I raised my leg and put it against his chest to push myself away from him. When he lunged, however, my spur caught in the breast collar and he dragged me down further from the safety of the bank.

I was only 20' from the edge of the bank but it took me 15 minutes to move myself close enough all the while trying to remain horizontal. There were small roots sticking out of the bank and I used them to gently draw myself out. At one point I was almost out when one of those roots broke and I fell back in.

Patty was running out of steam and not struggling any more. The saddle horn was all that was visible of the saddle. I found a 6' log which was 12' long from a nearby tree and dragged it to the edge of the quicksand. Sliding down the bank again there seemed to be a solid shelf to drop a log across the horses back about 6" behind the saddle horn. I shimmied forward on the log and pushing my hand into the quicksand was able to free the latigo. I use a quick release when saddling my horse for such an occasion as this. I soon had the back cinch free but couldn't reach the breast collar buckles. I used my knife to cut it off. That took some doing trying not to cut Patty with my razor sharp knife and keeping myself from rolling off the log.

I flung my canteen, pommel bags, and Winchester up onto the bank and dragged my saddle back to the little shelf at the base of the bank. Now Patty's head was the only thing above the quicksand and he had tilted sideways. After 4 1/2 hours with the help of 3 friends, my pickup truck and a logging chain we pulled Patty out. One of the farmers wanted to shoot him as he had lost several cattle in this stretch and they would die after 45 minutes from hypothermia or suffocation by constriction of their lungs.

Patty was a miracle. Pulling him up the bank it seemed his neck stretched an extra foot. When we took the chain off his eyes were rolled back in his head and he lay motionless. I began to rub him and massage him for 3 minutes and then he literally sprung up onto his feet and started trembling for a long time. I was afraid he might seize up so I loaded my tack into the truck and walked Patty 7 miles home. This is just a story to be warned of the dangers of quicksand but let me go back to the gear I wear.

In the U.S.A and Mexico the temperature in the desert can reach 115- 120F. Picking up something metal can burn your hands so be sure to travel with gloves. You will never use a lariat without gloves anyway so always have a good pair of leather ones with you.

The desert also has poisonous plants, thorns, snakes, spiders and scorpions. Have a plan in mind should you fall prey to any one of these.

Remember if you see someone struggling in the desert it is a crime not to lend a hand to help. That being said many a good Samaritan has been tricked by someone who was used as a decoy so they could rob them of their possessions and at times their lives.

Winter riding

6

Setting Up Camps

Each night of your trek you must find somewhere to set up camp. If you are using a horse trailer you need a place to pull off the road. Your ride may be just you and your horse and maybe a pack animal so you will need a spot to rest the horses and set up a tent. In the north and west of our continent are many areas to boon dock. Sometimes there are pullouts big enough for you to park and set up a small corral. My crew have set up camp off logging roads, oil well roads, abandoned farms, BLM land, and rest areas. When you get closer to populated areas it gets a little more difficult. Rodeo and fair grounds are great places but you must be able to get permission to stay there. This is why a crew is so helpful. While you are riding they are doing the leg work looking for a place to stay. There have only been a few times we have paid to stay at a camp ground. First, most don't want animals to mess up their camps and second, since I was raising money for charities and I was doing this ride by faith, there was no budget for accommodations. It was not unusual for people to stop us along our way to see what we were doing and offer us a place to stay at their farm or home. Many nights this is how we spent the evening and made wonderful friends along the way. You can go online to find other horse people who will allow you to stay at their facilities for free or a nominal charge. Net working with some of the people you meet will help as well, as many will know someone 20 or 30 miles up the road they can call to see if you can stay on their property. There are some great publications that can help you find places to camp. Look for books on state parks or online sites on boondocking. Our greatest asset was a book called *The Milepost*. This publication comes out every year and a crew actually drives every mile. We ran across their team on our travels and they questioned us about how helpful we found the information in their book. We were the first horse riders they had seen that far north. This publication documents mile by mile what you will find along all roads in Alaska, Yukon and northern British Columbia and Alberta.

Several important things to remember. Always get permission to stay on private property. If you cannot find someone to ask, ride on. When leaving camp the next morning, leave it as clean or cleaner than you found it. Pick up excess hay and droppings. When traveling on a reservation I suggest you get permission from the band office if you plan to stop anywhere other than road side rest areas. On one occasion in Arizona my crew pulled off on a large area at a four way stop that was littered with glass and garbage. It was on a reservation and although it was not the best place to camp it was all they could find. They got garbage bags and picked up the garbage and collected one feed bag full of glass. The corrals were set up and the horses out when someone dropped by who said it was not a safe area and offered for our team to come to their ranch about 5 miles away. The crew packed up, cleaned up the droppings and we ended up at a beautiful ranch with large paddocks for the horses. These kind people fed both horses and humans as well! If a pull off is all that is available check it for glass, wire and other things which could be harmful for your horse.

I am sad to say that some horse people do not have the proper etiquette in cleaning up after themselves and their animals and it gives a black eye for the rest of us. We were in northern British Columbia, when our crew was approached by a man who was very angry. He yelled at our crew for cleaning out our trailer in his gas station yard and leaving. We knew we had not done that and when we asked where his station was located we told him we had not been on that road but he would not believe us. Some other thoughtless horse person had made a mess and it caused this man to believe all horse people are the same.

One of the most useful things I found to take with us on our long ride were aluminum corral panels. They were so light my wife could easily lift them down off the side of the trailer where they were attached and within minutes could set up a large round pen. If a larger area was needed we would attach them to the side of the trailer or to an existing fence to give a bigger area for rolling and laying down.

Aluminum corral panels- quick and easy to set up

Another helpful idea for your horse to have more area for grazing is a portable electric fence system. I use a DD battery fencer that is light weight and compact. It is capable of electrifying 1/4 mile of fence at 4,000 volts. The DD batteries in constant use can last as much as 8 weeks. I use fibreglass posts that can easily fit into a rifle scabbard fastened to my saddle, or at base camp we use plastic, portable fence posts to allow for a large grazing area and place to lay down.

A word of caution: when fencing, know what noxious weeds to avoid and check for them as you set up. Also learn to look for other hazards such as ground hornet's nest, gopher and ground hog holes, game trails and chemical spray zones.

Our horse trailer had an outside light that we could switch on if there was a problem or noise outside we needed to investigate but we also kept a large lantern by the door if we had to run out to a horse in trouble

Camp setups along the way

7

Trailers

The standard three horse slant with a dressing/tack room, gooseneck is likely the most versatile, everyday trailer. For weekend rides you can sleep in the gooseneck and there is enough room inside to keep your gear dry if it rains. You may want to invest in a horse trailer with living quarters if your rides take you far from home for an extended period of time. The weekender living quarters generally have a shower, kitchenette, toilet and bed.

The trailer I used for our longest ride of 11,000 km or 6,700 miles was a Lakota trailer. I would highly endorse them. My wife and I lived in the trailer for over a year. They build them to be horse friendly and the living quarters are very comfortable. The trailer we used was the Charger from Lakota of Ohio as they sponsored our ride. It was a three horse slant with an eleven foot short wall. It had a full- sized fridge, exterior water faucet for filling horse water and lots of storage. We used that model from the Arctic Ocean to northern Montana when the owner of Lakota of Ohio, Gary Stites, brought me a new four horse slant with a 15 foot living quarters with a slide out that gave us so much more room. The overall length was 40 feet. My wife pulled it with a one ton, dual wheel pickup truck which was designed for such a task. It pulled like a dream.

Whatever trailer you choose there are certain safety issues you need to stay on top of. Wooden floors need to be checked often. I would recommend every 3 months to take a steel bar or pipe, pull up the rubber mats and tap the bar on the floor boards looking for soft spots or a dull thud instead of the sharp, crisp sound of solid wood. Replace the floor if it is questionable. On a trip through Colorado I met a man who had lost his horse due to a bad floor. While being trailered the horse fell through. This is a nightmare for those of us who love our horses.

Test your brakes regularly and know how to use your brake control. When travelling through the mountains let your transmission take some of the strain so you don't overheat your brakes. My pickup truck has an exhaust brake. It will save your brakes when you are on those long, steep mountain passes and downhill grades.

Electrical wires and lights need to be in good operating condition.

Make sure your tires are the type for trailers and not car tires. Car tires are designed differently, for a different purpose, than a trailer. The size prefix should start with S.T. For example, mine are S.T. 225/75 R 15.

Check the hitch regularly to ensure it is operating snuggly. Most trailers today are equipped with a breakaway battery control should your trailer come off your truck. It will engage your trailer brakes to bring it to a stop.

I chose a step up trailer over a ramp. I think it's good advice for every horse owner to ride in the back of the trailer with his horses at least once. It will give you a whole new appreciation for what your horse has to endure while traveling.

A word on loading: Don't make a big deal about loading and neither will your horse. If you have trouble loading and you finally coaxed your horse into the trailer and your helper quickly slams the door shut while you jump out, you will set yourself up for a difficult load next time. When you do this, your horse feels like you trapped him and since he is a flight animal he feels very uncomfortable. Go in with him and talk to him. He doesn't need any special treats- just your approval. He wants to please you. The best remedy is consistence and patience in loading day after day and soon it will become an easy, comfortable action. Horses that have been traumatized may require more time to trust you when it comes to loading. My horses walk in and out on command but it took daily loading and trailering to achieve that.

Open the side window first so when your horse steps in he does not feel confined. Once he has loaded, take the time to stand with him and stroke his neck till he is settled and quiet and then walk out and close the door.

I have used a variety of methods to load difficult horses. Some work on certain horses while others work with others. If you make the environment outside the trailer more uncomfortable than inside the trailer it may help. Remember the harsher method of loading is more likely to produce an injured horse or person- neither is a good idea.

Be sure the horse has good footing when backing out of the trailer. If he falls in icy conditions loading or unloading, you will have problems getting him to trust you again for a while. Teaching a new horse to load may be hard but not impossible.

Don't carry anything in the trailer where your horse is. I have seen folks stack gear around the horse's feet only to have things bounce or fall against the horse while driving on rough roads or making sharp turns. This only works against you and is unsafe for the horse.

I generally tie the horse in the trailer with a quick release knot but there are times I do not tie them at all. Remember if you tie your horse and he needs to cough, he will need to drop his head so give him enough room to do that but not enough to get a hoof or leg caught. Always carry a knife while trailering livestock in case an animal falls and you have to cut the lead rope.

The 40' 4 horse slant 15' short wall Lakota horse trailer given to us to use for our ride by Lakota of Ohio.

8

Food for the trail

Whether travelling for a weekend or a year you and your horse have to eat. Your horse will need a higher protein diet than normal. In certain climates and terrains grazing your horse may be limited. Be cautious about grazing near cities and also some rural areas where herbicide and pesticides may be sprayed on grassy areas. When tethering or hobbling your horse keep an eye out for noxious weeds and poisonous vegetation.

I like to use hay cubes when I am at base camp and I buy local hay if available. Most feed stores keep small supplies. I feed rolled oats and sweet feed with a red cell additive. I also add an electrolyte powder to the feed. In Utah, Arizona and Mexico we also carried a 65 gallon water tank as water was a prime commodity in desert areas.

Sometimes I will carry a nosebag for my horse with 2 quarts of grain for overnight. When I am on a longer journey I carry a soda bottle with grain so my horse can have a snack at lunch also.

For my own consumption I carry extra energy bars like Cliff bars, beef jerky and coffee. I may also take freeze dried foods and water purification tablets.

When on an overnight ride I like to buy eggs in a carton, which you can get in serval flavours, that taste good scrambled with bacon or ground beef. The best steak you will ever have will be roasted over an open fire on a stick or with a potato and vegetables in tin foil cooked in the campfire coals. When you get into a routine you can have your cooking fire and coffee as well as supper going in a half an hour. These times can be hampered by snow or rain. In the snow I lay 6 or 7, 3" diameter limbs on top of the snow then build my cook fire on top so the fire doesn't melt down into the snow and go out or tip my coffee pot over.

I have eaten rattle snake on the trail but I strongly recommend McDonald's drive through if you are near a town or city. In the north berries, mushrooms, puff balls, fiddleheads may be found as well as water cress in small streams. Apples, cherries and pears in lush areas and pecans in the lower U.S.A provide a sweet treat. Wild onions and Indian bread root as well as fishing will add to your diet. Check with local officials on varieties that can be fished for and if they are in season. Also check the local hunting and fishing regulations if you plan to shoot small game. It is likely you will need a small game permit and an upland game permit if you intend to shoot rabbit, grouse, pheasant etc.

Remember the rule of thumb for shooting and eating rabbits. Only do so in the months that have an "R" in the month's name. Months that don't have an "R" such as May, June July, and August are months to avoid eating rabbits as they often carry parasites during the warmer summer weather.

Some tree bark can be used for herbal teas but I prefer coffee.

Clean your canteen now and then with fresh clean water then put in an ounce of mouth wash and swish it around. Wait

5 minutes then rinse again with fresh water. This keeps the bacteria down.

I have used a product called Willard Water that I add to the horse's water at night. It helps to hydrate and prevent colic. I also use a small amount of sweet feed while travelling but I keep the molasses content low.

Remember when in bear country to cash your food away from camp and rope it into a tree. Try to not contaminate your clothing with food spills as that can also attract the bears. A grizzly can smell a dead carcass up to 20 miles away! I am not inferring that you smell like a dead carcass but keep your campsite clean.

Frogs make a good meal if you have the time to catch them. A sharp rap in the head will stun them and before long sizzling in your pan is the tender white meat people pay big dollars for in fancy restaurants.

You may want to avoid eating bananas and other strong foods as the smell does come out from your pores and attracts mosquitoes and black flies.

Try getting local honey to spread on tortillas. It is delicious. I especially like the mesquite honey from southern Arizona.

Trail mix and jerky are also convenient foods when blizzards or heavy down pours are a challenge to making a fire.

On my trip from Fairbanks to Mexico I lost 10 pounds but it wasn't for lack of food. Riding 10-12 hours a day will wear off any extra weight and your horse won't mind a bit.

Making a quick, efficient camp fire is easy if there are trees and the wood is dry. In northern Alaska for 100 miles there were no trees. It is permafrost in these areas and there is a limited amount of vegetation for your fire and your horse to eat. Some low shrubs that grow will burn but I usually pack a small bag of kindling and an egg carton as it will light quickly and doesn't blow out easily. A zippo lighter is also not affected by the wind as much as the smaller Bic lighters are. I also carry a flint stick and water proof matches if all else fails.

In hardwood forests look for birch trees as the bark is an excellent fire starter. Start the fire with small twigs making a teepee out of the twigs with your fire starter in the middle. Add larger branches, up to 2-3 inches in diameter next. If you have rain to contend with, find an area near a rock cut or over hang to keep the wind from blowing out your fire and the rain from dousing it. Check that your campfire is out before leaving your site. A good rule of thumb is to make sure it is cold to the touch.

Small, folding camp stove triangles are light weight and use a variety of fuels. I don't have one of these but they do seem like they would be a good idea.

Coffee break on the trail

9

Rider Etiquette

When travelling cross country you will need to obtain permission to ride on private land. This can be difficult but look for people in the area who may know the owner. There is plenty of crown land in Canada and BLM land in the U.S. that is available for public use. Some of these lands are leased out for livestock grazing or logging.

Always leave gates as you found them, whether open or closed. Many municipalities and cities still have written in their bylaws that horses and horse drawn carriages have the right of way on roads but check before assuming this is true.

You get to know your horse well when you travel hundreds of miles together and generally you know if he is going to leave droppings behind. It is good etiquette to know this before you head through town or stop at the coffee shop.

Pedestrians and bicyclist may be scary to your horse and your horse, in turn, may be intimidating to them, so yield the right of way and talk to them as you pass.

The times that I have gone into a restaurant to eat I always get a window seat so I can keep an eye on my horse. Watch for dogs which may bark and growl at the horse. My horse, General, doesn't pay them much mind but if they continue to irritate him he gets lined up and doesn't mind striking out to send the dog into tomorrow.

I like to take the saddle off when I stop for lunch to give my horse a break to breathe. This may not always be possible if you are tied up to a parking meter but at least loosen the cinch if you will be more than a half hour.

If carrying a firearm, particularly a leaver action, keep the chamber empty. I have heard of several bad injuries from cowboy's loaded firearms going off accidentally. Imagine having a loaded lever action, pushing it into your saddle scabbard and by doing so it cocks the hammer back. You now have a dangerous situation. Touching your trigger when pulling the rifle out of the scabbard will result in you shooting your horse.

People may want to touch or pat your horse but many do not know how to react around a horse. Make sure you keep control of your horse in case of a sudden scream, jump, or a child running around his rear or near his feet. Others may want to feed your horses a carrot or apple and may need coaching on how to do it correctly. The horse cannot always differentiate between a small carrot and a child's finger. I have had people want to share their chocolate bar with my horse but it is up to you to regulate what goes into your horse's mouth and chocolate can be toxic.

Keep your horse off golf courses, soccer fields and people's lawns. Be considerate of where you tie your horse if you go into a store or coffee shop.

I came out of a coffee shop one day to see General with all feet in the air. He was kicking and rearing against his lead rope. This was totally out of character for him. I did not realize I had tied him on top of a ground wasp nest and he stepped into it unleashing hundreds of angry wasps. There is no other way to help your horse but to get him out of the situation fast. That is why you must always carry a belt knife to cut the lead rope. A quick release knot will be so tight you will never get it undone fast enough in case of an emergency such as this.

A rule of thumb I use when riding on the road is to ride on the right side going uphill and on the left side going downhill. You can often hear the vehicles coming. When they approach you going up they can see you on the right side, however as you crest the hill you are then hidden and they may be surprised to come upon you as they come to the top of the hill. This could cause them to overreact. Traffic coming in the opposite direction plus a horse on the side of the road is potential for an accident.

I look for escape routes for my horse and me in the event of traffic. It is easier for me to move into the ditch than a vehicle.

When coming upon a bridge, stop and evaluate several things. If your horse is wearing steel shoes and the bridge is an open web, steel bridge, it is going to be very slippery for the horse. It will be strange for your horse to walk on steel and to see below. A truck passing is extremely loud.

I came upon on one of these obstacles on my trip where I had to go over a half mile long steel, open web bridge on a very busy highway. There was a rushing river 100 feet below the bridge as well. I chose easy boots for my horse's feet and crossed in the early morning before there was too much traffic. I got halfway across when a transport appeared and went whizzing by us at 70 mph. My horse never flinched. Another horse I have was not as calm. The noise and slippery bridge frightened her. I had to place my coat over her head and tuck her head under my arm and she allowed me to lead her over the river on the bridge.

Crossing open messed steel bridge

If you need to take your horse into a building like a school, store or shopping centre easy boots are a good idea as well as a drop bag to catch any droppings. You will leave with a more friendly and less aggravated janitorial staff.

Have a plan in advance if you come across other horses. In many parts of the Americas there are small herds of wild horses. A gelding won't draw much attention from them but if you are on a stud or mare you may be confronted. A mare in season will draw awareness from a herd, but a lariat or bull whip will keep a stallion at bay till you pass. Riding a stallion may cause the herd's stallion to challenge yours and you will need to get more aggressive in passing. I have used my lariat and made lots of noise and charged my stallion at him. The other stallion seeing you charge with a lariat and hearing all the noise will think you are trying to rope him and will break off and gather his herd and be gone with the wind.

Leave the wild life alone while traveling. Enjoy seeing them and maybe get some pictures for your travel diary.

I wish someone had written this book for me before I did my trips. I recall in North Carolina riding a friend's green broke horse. I decided to rope a Canada goose that was honking at us. He was likely protecting his wife and kids but he was being a pest to me as he hissed and bluff charged my horse, who by the way, had never seen a Canada goose before. I made a loop and tried to rope the bird but he flew into the middle of the coil and directly at the horse. He hit the horse with his feet and wings square in the forehead then he went straight for me knocking my hat off. I hate to lose my head gear as I had $200.00 tucked into the hat brim. My hat hit the ground and out bounced my bank roll which was quickly caught by the wind. The horse had gone into a bucking and crow hopping frenzy which sent this cowboy to the ground. I was groping for my reins and my hat at the same time as I watched the wind scatter my bills. The wind had been knocked out of me and I was clutching my hat and the reins of the horse that was still pitching. I looked skyward in humility as that goose made several passes over us. Now I have never seen a Canada goose laugh but I expected it would look a lot like that one.

10

Your Support Team

Choose your support team carefully. It is best if you know them well and be sure everyone knows your guidelines. You may have an I.T. person at home to monitor and evaluate social media for you. This was very helpful to me on my 2014-2015 and 2016 rides.

Cell phone and internet connection will not always be available on a daily or maybe even a weekly basis so it is very helpful to have a computer savvy person willing to help from your home base. They can give updates as to your location by way of a Spot, G.P.S. or Google earth with the topographical views of the terrain. My Spot had an emergency button, that when depressed, would activate an S.O.S. to my support team or local emergency personnel. This would be used if you had a wreck and were in serious danger, perhaps a broken leg or back. You are able to be tracked via satellite to within 1 meter of your location. It is not to be used indiscriminately as the cost to you can be enormous as you must pay the rescue teams.

On my first long ride my support team was my wife, Nancy, and my three boys, who were very young. The boys helped with feeding of horses, setting up camp, corral panels, fishing as well as keeping up their school work. We had no cell phones to stay in contact. Pay phones in a town or village were our connection with the outside world. There was no G.P.S, only a compass and map.

Nancy would drive ahead 20 or 30 miles and set up camp. I would ride until I found their camp.

Since we were headed south, if I rode the back country and came onto the main road I would go south and my family would eventually find me. If we missed our connection I would ride into the next village and leave a message with the local information centre and continue riding. On one occasion I missed camp by 10 miles but I thought I was north of my family when in fact I was south and ended up 100 miles south before they found me.

My oldest son, Matt, became adept at tracking my horse and could tell if I was ahead of them if I stayed on the shoulder of the road. I was using easy boots on the front feet and steel plates on the back so I was easy to track.

My family was the best support team I could ever want. We learned to lean on each other, we worked together, and each of us had our own responsibilities. We grew stronger as a family in faith and endurance. Twenty-two years later we still talk about our ride for missions.

Your support team can help with local information and securing feed for your horse as they travel ahead. They can help locate water in desert areas as well. The crew also looked after my press appointments and lined up reporters that wanted to interview me when I got to town.

Often you will have volunteers that want to join your team. It is best to sit down and go over camp rules or guidelines for all to follow. In my camp I do not allow alcohol or drugs. We had a lot more fun with a Bible, song books and guitar around a camp fire. Great memories were made sitting around the fire as a team watching the northern lights, a lunar eclipse, the constellations or listening to the night sounds and watching fireflies across the meadows.

My team was a blessing to me in the Yukon when I rode into camp with a broken shoulder and a torn elbow after a fall. My horse needed attention and my team were all over it like the pros they were.

It does help if your team speaks the same language! In Mexico I had a wonderful family take over at the U.S. border as my support team. They spoke no English, and I, no Spanish. In the next 1,200 miles of riding through Mexico I learned some Spanish and my Mexican family learned some English. We became close as friends even though there was a language barrier.

The Mexican family that was my crew while riding through their country

11

Dealing with Discouragement

You may face many nay sayers as you begin to plan your trip, but you will find just as many who will be a huge encouragement to you. Surround yourself with positive people. Your support team should be your greatest asset as far as encouragement.

I have found my faith in God has sustained me through what could have been a game stopping blow, had I not had the joy of knowing God's love and leading in my life.

One thing that will help you, is to ride for purpose not necessarily just for pleasure. Pleasure riding is great but it is just that; pleasure. Riding long distances will have you experience foul weather, extreme temperatures, solitude, little sleep and being ever alert- it is not what one would consider a Saturday afternoon ride. Riding for a purpose will help drive you to completion.

I ride predominantly to help widows and orphans in less fortunate countries than our own. Over the years I have travelled to where they live, eaten in their homes, laughed and cried with them and I now see they are real people like you and me. They have real names, real families and live in a real place. In North America we live in a bubble and are oblivious to the rest of the world. Only 10% of the world's population live like we do. When I ride, I see their faces, I feel their hunger and I share their plight. It helps to keep me in the saddle to think that maybe my horse and I can make a difference. When discouragement comes, and it will, step back and look at the bigger picture as to why you are out there. If it's for adventure, that's good. If it's to help others, that's good. If it's for experience that's good and if it's for you that's OK, too. Just remember the reason for your journey. If it is for yourself, adventure or experience you will be tempted to throw in the towel when it gets tough, however, if you are out there for others it will sustain you through the hardships and keep you in the saddle.

Remember whether it is 50 miles or 5,000 miles all you need to be successful is taking one step at a time. There will be days you will feel like you wish you were somewhere else- like Philadelphia, but you will find within yourself the measure of the person you are by staying the course with your feet in the stirrups and your hands on the reins.

By the way, I've never been to Philadelphia, it just seemed at times anywhere would have been a better place to be than where I was. Besides, the name "Philadelphia" means "brotherly love"- seems like it might be a nice place. Perhaps one day I'll visit there.

After one year and four days in the saddle I rode up in front of my destination point in Mismaloya, Mexico. The orphanage I ended at was located on the hill to the right. Here is a high five with my friend, Gary Stites, of Lakota Ohio, who rode several times with me throughout my ride. We are followed by a group of cowboys from the local cattle men's association.

APPENDIX

Below you will find some of the distributors of products that I have found beneficial for my horse, myself and my riding.

Easy Boots- www.easycareinc.com
Circle Y Saddles- www.circley.com
Ken McNabb saddles- www.kenmcnabb.com
The Milepost- www.themilepost.com
Lakota of Ohio Horse Trailers- www.lakotaofohio.com
Kenetrek Insulated Cowboy Boots-www.kenetrek.com
Willard's Water- www.drwillard.com
Bit less Bridles www.nuturalhorse.com

Len's website-lencrow.ca
Follow Len on Facebook Ride for Missions

Printed in the United States
By Bookmasters